From My Ashes, Flowers Will Bloom

Poetic Singh

Copyright © 2015 Poetic Singh

All rights reserved.

ISBN-13:978-1512096538

"The scars always remain, we just get better at hiding them."

Poetic Singh

DEDICATION

This is dedicated to my mother, Surinder Kaur and my father, Kesar Singh. Both have gone through such hardship to raise the three of us and without their sacrifice, guidance and firm hand, we would not be the men that we are now. To them, I dedicate every word in this book. Without them, I am nothing. For this, I thank you mum and dad.

I love you both with all my heart.

CONTENTS

Acknowledgment   i

Anger   Page 1

Sadness   Page 27

Regret   Page 47

Love   Page 63

Contemplation   Page 93

Waheguru   Page 125

About   Page 137

ACKNOWLEDGMENT

I'd like to express my thanks to everyone that has helped me in the creation of this book. The ones that have stood by me in my hours of weakness. Without your support, love and encouragement, I doubt this would be a reality. You have all helped me in creating something from the depths of my soul and my heart. For that, I am eternally grateful.

My friends, you are my family.

Anger

I'll cut you out like a cancer
That's been growing inside of me
I don't care if it's the right answer
I'll be fine without you
Just you wait and see

I've lost my appetite for your words
They left a bitter taste
My hunger for you is gone today
My time was all a waste
I'm living for me now
I'm happy in my own space

If I could speak my mind
The choice of words would be unkind
Words of sorrow and hurt
Are what you'll hear when my heart erupts

Suffocating in silence
Gasping, gasping for air
Who'd have known it could be so violent
Trying to reach out for you
And finding no one was there...

This bitter pill is so hard to swallow
But drink up my dear
You have nothing to fear
Let's make a toast tonight
Your end is in sight

I don't have the stamina
To keep up with your drama
You run your mouth
Talking about vanity and glamour

You belittle
You shout
You scream
Have you ever thought about your words
And what they all could mean

What's the point in talking
When I've said all I need to say
Your intent is always in walking
Far, far away...

Our friendship
Has sunk to the bottom of the sea
A long voyage ended too soon
Never did I think this would be
Stuck between the sea and the Moon
Our end has come too soon

Would you be happy
If I drowned in my own tears
After all you've done to me
Only I can know these fears...

No takers, that's a shame
Would it be better if I was plain
Or the same
As every other Sardar you've known
I am unique
Now watch my lips, as my words flow

Why is your world full of so much hate
You seem to be fine with playing God
You persecute and perpetrate
An almighty, racial tirade
Yet you, are the one that is odd

When you look at me
What do you choose to see
The real man I am
Or what you'd like me to be
I am not here to merely please you
I am here to simply do
What He asks me to

When you chose to self-destruct
You took out all of those around you
Perhaps that wasn't your intention
Ripped through me and tore me in two

Today is deceptively cold
Much like your heart
Always was a bitter reminder
Manipulation
Was your chosen craft

When your demise is near
That's when the vultures close in
They can taste your fear
Now they will consume your sin

Fools will always suffer
Foolish like no other
Blindly believing in faith and love
Left seething
By the ones they trust
Left out in the cold
Hearts turning to rust

With you I tried
I gave it my all
If only you'd talked to me
Instead you watched me fall
What can be said
I thought you'd call, just one call

I'm wounded so you best watch your back
Come near me and my instinct is always to attack
Betrayed by friend and foe
Step back when you hear a lion roar

Why am I too blind to see
You're not the right one for me...

You don't understand
My tongue is sharp like a knife
The words that I say will cut you deep
This isn't a song
I'm not here to give you a hand
Now what are you going to do with your life
Are you going to lead or follow like a sheep
Best think quickly
Life doesn't last very long

Tears soaked into the fabric
Never to wash away the stain
Today came a realisation
That will forever hold a haunting pain
You were an idol held so dear
Now she hides the gifts of black and blue
The father she lovingly looked up to
Now she cuts herself on the love she once knew

Don't promise things you won't keep
For my time, and loyalty
Are not cheap
Don't call me friend
When it's only selfish deeds
That you intend
Don't call me friend…

I'll push you away
Before you get the chance
If life has taught me one thing
When it comes to love, it's an awkward dance

Sadness

The atmosphere has changed
There's something not right in this house
No words fill these rooms now
Acting like everything is okay
In this house
We have forgotten to pray...

I write from my Mind
Body and Soul
With only one goal
To let these feelings out
Before my spirit and heart
Head south

Grief and sadness
Motivate like no other emotion
The pain of loss is so great
Inside us all it creates such intense commotion
Sorrow and loss
Invoke an unhealthy notion

I want to be home
I want to be in your loving embrace
Make me forget all my pain
Fill my heart with happiness
Right now it's an empty space

Never have I felt more alone than I do now
Invisible to everyone
Far from everything
Missing you more than you'll ever know

Hung up like curtains
Hung up on hang ups
Helpless, careless and shameless
Trying to ascertain, through pain
Why you distain my thoughts

Heavy thoughts
Thoughts which scar my mind
Thoughts that are unkind
Thoughts that have made me blind
Clarity has become hard to find
Out of sight
Out of mind
A gift or a sign
Forever searching for the sublime

The rain showers descend upon me
Cleansing my thoughts
Drops dance on my body
My tears are lost in the rain
Washing away this mortal pain

Father, I am not ready
To let you go
Father, I am not ready
To sit upon your seat
Father, I am not ready
I am cannot admit defeat
Father, I am not ready
To carry this burden on my own
You must pull through
For all of our sakes
Father, I am sorry
Sorry I am not a stronger son
My heart breaks

Remember not to forget the fallen
And what they stood for
Countless died
So that we might live on
A father never to see his son

Remember to be silent
For the dead
For they cannot speak
For what they saw was violent
Forever tears shall be shed
All we seek now is peace

The truth can be brutal
For what they saw was horrific
Killing upon killing
I cannot be more specific
Lest we forget

Our house
Is an empty home
Without you here
At a time when we need you near
Alone we sit
Realising our biggest fear

I'm sat in my father's chair
How odd a feeling is this
Once he sat here
A captain commanding his ship
In a blink of an eye, gone with one slip

Today I am a void
A shell of what once stood
No tears to shed
Hope is gone
All that remains is a vacant room

Freedom

Overwhelmed with emotion
Sadness, anger and grief
The day he took his final breath
That was his only relief

Happiness is a drop
In the vast ocean of sadness
Tiny ripples
Of a time spent lost at sea of life

Today I held your hand
If only my grip had been tighter
Praying and hoping for your safe return
Father, you are my soldier, you are my fighter
I am a lonely loving son

Regret

I can quench my hunger with food
I can quench my thirst with water
I cannot quench my need for love
I will always feel empty without you

I'm woven together
Like strands of fabric
When one becomes frayed
You pull at it
Then I tear apart
From one end
To the start

I don't remember the last time I was happy
I mean truly happy
Maybe I've never had that moment of bliss
I'm still waiting for that one wish

Packed like sardines
On this bus
People scurry around like ants
Everyone's always in such a rush
Take your time
Before it runs out
Hush

Time that has been lost
Can be made up
Memories made in the past
Shall never be forgotten
For our time shall come again
We wait for the 'when'

Always wanting what you can't have
Always left wanting more
A disease with no cure
Now seeps in through every pore
Left alone in my last moments
My heartbeat begins to slow
So many things I hoped to be
Now fades my glow

Impatiently waiting
For everyone
Continually debating
Should I wait or get up and leave
I am forever waiting

Suffer, suffer
On your own
Because of your actions
Suffer suffer, all alone

The caring voices fade
As sharply as they were once audible
Now the water is too deep to wade
I am the one left in the middle

Why would you want to commit suicide
Deep down is it really that bad inside
I'm trying to help you
Please don't hide from me
You are all that I see

If only I was good enough
To wipe away your tears
If only I was good enough
To help you escape your fears
If only I was good enough
To wind back the years

My mind is strong
Yet my body is weak
Entombed in this prison of flesh
My future is so bleak
The One that can give me peace
His voice has now ceased

I won't leave intentions of me
Late at night I'll slip away out of sight
To hold back my dark
It will take all of my bright

Love

If I could take your pain
And make it mine I would
If God can do this for you
I think he should
I love you more
Than any son ever could

Hearing your voice brings it all back
I should be thankful for that
I can still hear your voice
It starts a commotion, stirs emotion…

With you by my side
I could live anywhere in the world
No matter what we face
There would always be a bright side

You can be my muse
If you, choose, to be so
My inspiration, the instigation
Of ideas and happiness
Not a mere irritation
But please do not confuse
For love is my condition

Deep within me, tortured by guilt and fear
All I wish for you is freedom from pain and suffering
But I'm too selfish to let you go
I am sorry for loving you so

My mother's love spans
Across the ocean to me
Her love is timeless
Her love is pure
Her love is boundless
Her love is a mother's love

Everything good I have came from you
Yet still I question you
I cannot help myself
I wish I could
I really do love you
It is true

Mother, mother
High above the clouds you soar
As I lay my head down for slumber
I pray you safely reach Scotland's shores
For I wish to feel your sweet embrace
Once more
Mother, mother
Forevermore

As small as my heart is
It holds a love so magnificent and pure
You are all I've ever wanted
Even now with a distance so far I am sure

Mother, oh mother
How honoured I am
To be the one you call son
Now I stand before you a man
What have you not done for me
You still continue to be so selfless
Giving me a love
A mother's love so flawless

Dance like no one's watching
Sing like no one's listening
Be who you are
Just be
As the winds are from the mountains to the sea
And be who you are truly meant to be
Happy and carefree

Be proud
Of your skin
For what it holds within
Is so delicate
Fragile and thin
It wraps around your bones
Ever so tightly
Your beautiful tones

Body beautiful

Don't let anyone define who you are

Mold your own image in this life

Your beauty will always set you apart...

Body beautiful
You cannot wear the words
That people will label you in
So choose your own style
Wear your own skin

Love you, for you
Only then
Others will, love you
For you
It's the only way
To be true
Ultimately this
Will get you through

Your beauty radiates from within
Your glow is warm and kind
Brings a smile to my face
From you happiness radiates
Simply smile

Your tears flow so freely
This comes from you trying to mask your fear
Let it go father
Let go of your fear
You are not alone
You are the one we hold so dear

Be my queen
From this day until our last
Healing scars of the heart
Erasing pain from the past
This is cheers to our new start

You are my little shadow
Never a step or two away
Beautifully you mimic everything I do
My heart brims with joy when I'm with you

I still remember that day
You held me so tight
Even now at a distance so great
Your love is too strong to fight
You're pulling me back now
Within my sight

Be my ship

I'll be your sail

Steady as we go, navigating this turbulent sea

Slow and sure we plot our course

In this unforgiving ocean my dear

It's just you and me

Wishing I could be a big brother
And hold my little brother tight
Give him the biggest hug possible
And tell him all will be alright

The bonds we share
Are a great burden on our fragile hearts
Invisible ties hold us together
Even time and distance cannot keep us apart

Another year older
Becoming bolder
Thank you
For being my shoulder
Happy birthday James
Please don't ever change

My body aches
And hungers for your touch
I long for that day to be now
Am I asking for too much
I now bide my time
Waiting for a sign

You speak my heart and mind better than I
If only I could be rid of these blinkers
I'd open my eyes and see
The beauty all around me

My love for you remains the same
Unlike continually changing seasons
Even though over time
You keep giving me reasons
To turn and walk away
With a love so strong
I'd do anything to stay

Your love flows over me
Like a tidal wave
Only now after all this time
I feel like someone you could save

Contemplation

Hope is tomorrow
Hope is loved ones
Hope is sorrow
Hope is caring
Hope is me
Believing in you
Hope is us
Seeing it through

We are all perfectly
Imperfect
We are uniquely
The same
We are colourful
Never mundane
Your worry is my worry
Nothing about you is plain

I may not be
The greatest poet
My time is yet to come
Funny thing is nobody knows it
I'll shine bright
With all my light
Before your eyes
I'll spread my wings and take flight

Music soothes my soul like no other
It holds me tight
Like a warm embrace from a mother
In that solitary moment everything feels so right

Her voice is music to my ears
Those sweet red lips intoxicate
Her smell it enchants
If only now I could recall her taste
Dancing that eternal dance

It is but a dream to know
You feel the same way
If there was evidence
Even a little care
Then it would make sense
Perhaps I'd be willing to dare

When I see you
The tears of joy
Will drown all the sadness and pain
I'll be reborn
I'm coming home to continue my reign

Night after night
I pour my heart onto paper
Hoping these words
Will give me a bigger purpose
Help me understand the point of life
Surely there's more to this
Than the mundane noise
The daily struggle with pain
Hear me, hear me
I listen well too
Although I am dumb
I am not your fool

Happiness breeds happiness
Sadness breeds sadness
Be happy and pay no mind to others
For my happiness is your happiness
Today I am happy

What can one do
When feeling so alone
Sat here glued to the phone
Staring at the screen
Trying to work out
What it all could mean...

Walking on pavements
Trying to avoid every crack
For you don't want to be the one
Who breaks your mothers back

We seek solace in the ones we meet
The ones we care for
In the ones we love
Like no other they give us inner peace
Love has become our drug

Beauty is everywhere
Take a minute to enjoy it
Taste the air you breathe
Feel the light you see

It's like a drug addiction
Hard to get free
What happens if you don't want to be free
Then what do you do
Who do you become
What will you be

Even in death there is a purpose
Even in death there is beauty
Close your eyes
And let your mind's eye see the world
Perhaps then you will see it in a different light

If only I could read your mind
I'd be better for you
If only I knew what you wanted
Better yet, if only you knew

If I can't hold you at this time
I'll put my message in a bottle
And send it on its way
I hope my words reach the one that's true
Carried along on the oceans waves
You'll know I did what I had to do
I said all I had to say

I haven't seen a sunrise in so long
If only you could see what I see
Perhaps
You'd be as amazed as me
As beauty rises before me

I wear my mask
Like our beautiful Earth wears her atmosphere
To mask all
That I loathe and fear

Why, given that we are all human
Then is humanity so rare
Why do some have a burden to bear
And others sit idly by and show no care
Human rights are for all humans
We are all the same
We pretend to be better
How is that fair

I write because I feel
I want you to feel what I feel
So you know that it's real
Perhaps that way, I can start to heal
That's the only true appeal

An ocean and eight hours keep us apart
When my day ends, your day starts
A heavy burden on my heart

It's never too late to follow your heart
Too often I see two souls part
Worrying about what is to unfold
Time passes and we all grow old

I thirst to hear your voice
I yearn to see your face
Maybe one day soon we will again embrace
Perhaps just for old times' sake

Beauty is everywhere
Take a minute to enjoy it
Taste the air you breathe
Feel the light you see

The body lingers
As the mind floats free
Away from thoughts of sadness
The truth is all it can see

Time for reflection
On what has passed
Way back from the inception
It's hard to see why things don't last...

As soon as you start to believe
It will all flow away
The pain will start to alieve
No one will be able to hold your love at bay

The train slithers along the snaking track
Making sharp turns and stopping abruptly
Patiently I wait for my stop
The grind has begun again

Where there is judgment
There is also acceptance
Not everyone you meet
Is to blame
We are all diverse
We are not all the same
Remember we are all unique

Waheguru

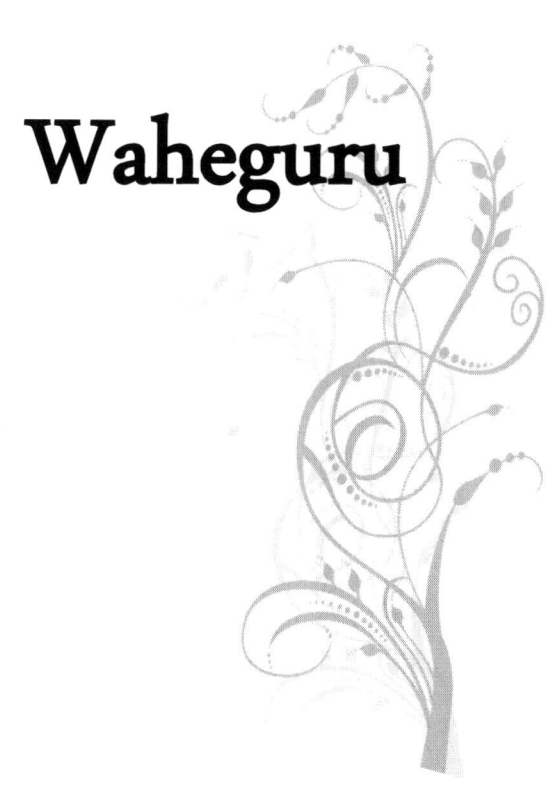

My soul smiles
As it finds peace
Found in Waheguru's house
All negative thoughts begin to cease
My soul smiles
As it finds peace

I woke up truly happy today
What can I say
Waheguru spoke
And has shown me the way
Take it day by day
All will be okay...

I see things today that make me smile
It's a rare sight
But you'll see me for miles
My Dastar and smile shine bright

As long as Waheguru's
Light
Shines bright
In us all
We will continue this
Fight
For justice and
Human rights

We are all the same
We're not pointing fingers
Trying to blame
We want acknowledgment
For our suffering and pain
The ones we've lost
Gone without a name

The majestic saffron
Waves in the wind of His glory
A symbol of the Khalsa
And a celebration of His Victory
Long may it rise above us all
A reminder of freedom
Here we reside happy
This is His Kingdom

In His house
I find peace
In His house
My earthly pain begins to cease
In His house
The silence overtakes
In His house
My soul awakes
In His house
I am compelled to pray
In His house
I have all the right words to say...

About

Born in Glasgow in 1983 to a modest Sikh family, Jaswinder Singh and his parents were visiting Punjab in 1984. They left and moved back to Glasgow a few days before the assassination of Indira Gandhi and the devastating Sikh pogroms.

The eldest of three brothers, he was educated in Scotland and spent the majority of his early adult life working in and around Glasgow.

In 2014 he moved to Canada for a year and it was during this time that family illness struck. Being so far away from home, he found that he needed an outlet for the emotions he was experiencing.

Gradually he turned from writing blogs to writing poetry. Over the next few months, he created some beautiful yet heart wrenching poems that covered not only his family concerns but also situations around him and those he found himself in.

From love, to hate, self-harm and manipulation of the heart, no topic was ever off limits. A good son, a good Sikh and a trustworthy friend, one cannot help but be moved by the emotions shared through his exquisite words.

James Ji

For more information on Poetic Singh, please visit his website at
www.poeticsingh.com

Thank you again
Poetic Singh

Front Cover	Copyright © Olga Lullis
Flower Stem & Leaf Black	Copyright © PixGood
Floral Vine Illustration	Copyright © Gintaras Svalbonaz
Image of Author	Copyright © TurbanEsque

Printed in Great Britain
by Amazon.co.uk, Ltd.,
Marston Gate.